Righteousness to Parents!

by Umm Assad

Find the radio in every scene!

This book belongs to

Abdul-Ahad

This book is not intended as a replacement for seeking knowledge. The reader is advised to take full responsibility for safeguarding their knowledge and understanding of Tawheed by regularly referring to authentic sources such as the Qur'an, Sahih ahadith, studying books of Scholars and their trusted students and other than that in the matters relating to his/her religion (Islam).

ISBN-13: 978-0-9957607-6-9
ISBN: 0995760764

Author: Umm Assad Bint Jamil Mohammed
Book Design: Umm Assad Bint Jamil Mohammed
Published on: 2018CE/1440H

ummassadpublications.com

Bismillahir-Rahmanir-Raheem. Indeed, all praise is for Allah. We praise Him; we seek His help, and we seek His Forgiveness. We seek refuge with Allah from the evil of our own souls and the consequence of our actions. Whomsoever Allah guides, nobody can misguide and whomsoever Allah misguides nobody can guide. I testify that none has the right to be worshipped except Allah alone, He has no partners, and I testify that Muhammad is His slave and Messenger.

DEDICATION

The following script was based on a true story. It was inspired by a lecture about being dutiful to parents. The lecture was given by Shaikh Muhammad al-Aqeel which was translated by Abu Hakeem Bilal Davis (may Allah preserve them both). The lecture can be found on salafisounds.com

I ask Allah to make us righteous parents,
to let our children be the coolness of our eyes
and to bestow His Mercy upon our parents!
Ameen.

Umm Assad

One day a little girl was playing in the living room with her toys. She heard her parents listening to a lecture about being dutiful to parents.

When the lecture ended, the little girl's father called her to sit with him.

'Yes abbi,' she replied.
She sat down beside her parents as they told her how much they loved her. Then her father asked,

In the Quran,
Allah سبحانه وتعالى has ordered us to worship Him alone.
Then right after that, He mentions to be righteous to our parents.[1] Especially when we're grown!

The Prophet Muhammad صلى الله عليه وسلم said, 'The best deeds are the prayer and to pray them all on time. Then be kind to both our parents.'[2] Don't make them sad or cry![3]

We have so many blessings that we can never count.[4]
Our parents are the greatest blessings that we are honoured to have around.

One day a man asked the Prophet ﷺ
'Who should we be more dutiful to?'

He ﷺ said,
'Your mother, then your mother, then your mother,
and then your father too.'[5]

So don't waste your time on evil things; they will never help you. Bad company, deeds, and computer games can only harm you or misguide you.

Did you know that you can never fully repay your parents, not even a breath our mother cried?[6]
She went through the hardship of carrying you, giving birth to you and staying up with you all night.[7]

Your mother taught you how to walk and talk and lost a lot of sleep. As you became big and strong, she became tired and weak.

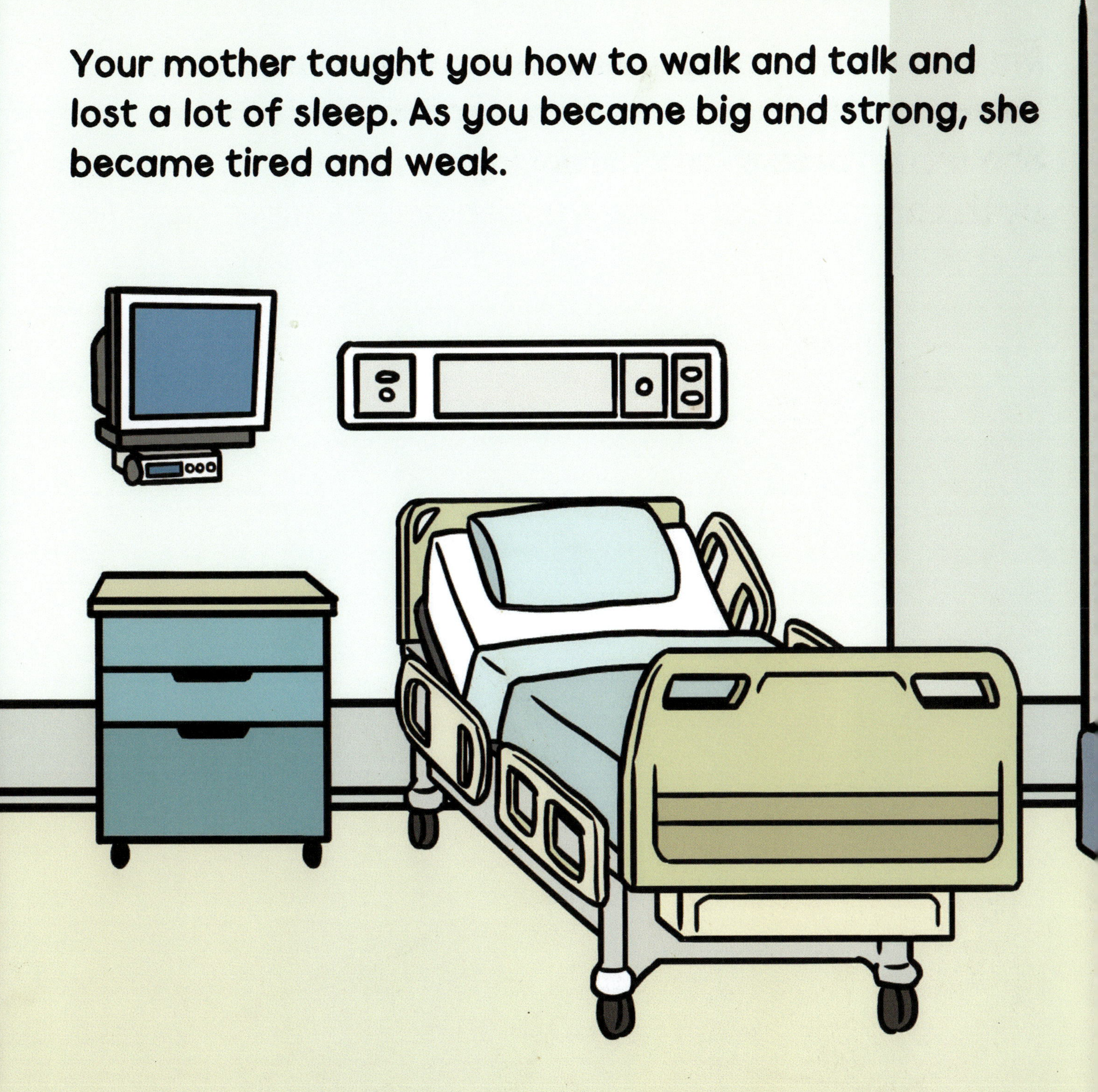

There are some ways we can repay our parents but not everybody can. Can we free them both from slavery or better yet invite them to Islam?[8]

We must obey our parents, as long as their orders are good. [9] Respect them whether Muslim or not. Just as a Muslim should. [10]

Allah ﷻ loves those who are kind and fair even if others are not. [11] These are the characteristics of a Muslim. So be fair no matter what.

Righteousness to parents can help us get to Jannah.
I hope one day we can. [12] Disobedience to parents can
lead us to Jahannam; a place no one can stand.

There are so many righteous deeds that our parents love to hear and see. Have the best of manners and don't forget to say 'thank you' and 'please'.

When your parents enter a room, stand up straight with a smile and say, 'Asalaamu alaykom ya ummi wa abbi, how are you today?'

Greet us with a handshake or kiss, just like the Prophet's ﷺ daughter. Offer your seat and we'll do the same, even when we are getting older. [13]

It's from good manners to help out with the housework without expecting a reward or treat.

Always remember to serve your parents before yourself and let them be the first to drink or eat. [14]

Do lots of good deeds that will benefit you; this will make us proud of you. Seek knowledge, pray and recite the Quran too. There's so much you can do.

Whenever you want or need something, ask nicely for permission. If we say 'no', don't frown or moan but forgive and show your full submission. [15]

Be grateful for the things you have because it could be a whole lot worse.
Some people have no family, home or a penny in their purse. Others have no education, food and no access to a scholar or nurse.

Remember to thank your mother and father for all the provisions that they give.
Allah ﷻ blesses us with so much wealth; we can give a lot away as gifts.

Here are a few examples of how we can be righteous to our parents:

Always:

1. Show excellent manners
2. Obey your parents in all things good
3. Speak with humility/shyness (all of shyness is good)
4. Use loving words; 'Yes mother, I'm at your service'
5. Be truthful
6. Serve their needs
7. Do lots of good deeds
8. Wait your turn
9. Be good when your parents are present/absent
10. Make your parents laugh and smile

Never:

1. Show anger or unhappy faces
2. Disobey unless there is harm involved
3. Avoid or ignore
4. Argue
5. Shout or scream
6. Lie or hide anything
7. Do bad deeds
8. Interrupt unless it's an emergency
9. Make your parents angry or sad
10. Cut ties

'Labyaka ya ummi!'
'Na'm ya ummi!'

Finally, always remember that your parents love you and would do anything to keep you happy and safe. Their supplication to Allah سُبْحَانَهُ وَتَعَالَى is accepted so ask them to supplicate for you and say, [16]

'O my Lord, have mercy on
my parents as they had mercy
on me when I was small.' [17]

We ask Allah سُبْحَانَهُ وَتَعَالَى to give our parents the best rewards in both worlds and make us dutiful.

Ameen!

Glossary

Allah – The one true God
Quran – Revelation/Speech from Allah
Sunnah – Revelation sent from Allah to Prophet Muhammad, Prophet's example, teachings, etc
Islam – To worship Allah alone and not join partners with Him
Muslim – The one who submits to Allah alone
Asalaamu alaykom – Peace be upon you
Ya ummi wa abbi – O my mother and my father
Jannah – Paradise
Jahannam – Hell-Fire
Ameen – O Allah answer the supplication

صلى الله عليه وسلم - Sallallahu alaihi wasallam – May the peace and blessings of Allah be upon him (referring to the Prophet Muhammad)

 - Subhanahu wa Ta'ala- May He be glorified and exalted (referring to Allah)

Endnotes

1. Quran: Surah 17, Ayah 23 – Translator: Muhsin Khan
2. Hadith: English Translation of Sahih Muslim, Volume 1, Book of Faith, Hadith [256] 140 - (85), Page 173-174
3. Hadith: Al-Adab Al-Mufrad (Imam Bukhari) by UK Islamic Academy: Chapter 9, Hadith 19
4. Quran: Surah 14, Ayah 34/Surah 16, Ayah 18
5. Hadith: Sahih Al-Bukhari (Arabic-English), Volume 8, Book of Good Manners, Hadith 5971
6. Hadith: Al-Adab Al-Mufrad (Imam Bukhari) by UK Islamic Academy: Chapter 6, Hadith 11
7. Quran: Surah 31, Ayah 14/ Surah 46, 15-16
8. Hadith: Al-Adab Al-Mufrad (Imam Bukhari) by UK Islamic Academy: Chapter 6, Hadith 10. Hadith: English Translation of Sahih Muslim, Volume 6, Virtues of the Companions, Hadith [6396] 158 - (2491), Pg. 357
9. Quran: Surah 29, Ayah 8
10. Hadith: Sahih Al-Bukhari (Arabic-English), Volume 8, Book of Good Manners, Hadith 5978-5979
11. Quran: Surah 60, Ayah 8
12. Sunan An-Anasa'i compiled by Imam Hafiz Abu Abdur Rahman Ahmad bin Shu''aib bin 'Ali An-Nasa'i, Translated by Nasiruddin al-Khattab [Volume 3, The Book of Funerals, Hadith 1877, Page 46-47]
13. Hadith: Al-Adab Al-Mufrad (Imam Bukhari) by UK Islamic Academy: Chapter 443, Hadith 971
14. Hadith: Sahih Al-Bukhari (Arabic-English), Volume 3, Book of Sales, Hadith 2215
15. Quran: Surah 2, Ayah 216
16. Hadith: Al-Adab Al-Mufrad (Imam Bukhari) by UK Islamic Academy: Chapter 17, Hadith 32 – (Hasan Hadith)
17. Quran: Surah 17, Ayah 24

Note: For more references, please refer to authentic sources.

ABOUT THE AUTHOR:

Umm Assad has had a great love for helping others since early childhood. She has worked for both the elderly and preschool. Umm Assad also enjoys seeking knowledge and writing to express her lessons in life. Over the years, this passion has seen her create unique books, children's educational resources and even poetry of which some she now enjoys sharing.

Some of Umm Assad's best-selling titles are 'Allah is My Lord' and 'The Prophet Muhammad'.

You can contact Umm Assad where you can also download your free 'Islamic Activity Pack' to use alongside her books:

Websites: ummassadpublications.com, ummassadhomeschool.com
Twitter: ummassadpubs
Instagram: ummassad.pubs
Facebook: ummassadpubs
Youtube: ummassadpublications

ummassadpublications.com

'Take Pride in Authenticity'

Printed in Poland
by Amazon Fulfillment
Poland Sp. z o.o., Wrocław